The MAILBOX®

The Education Center®

Math
Step-by-Step
CENTERS

W9-BZW-362

Grades K–1

38 easy-to-use center activities

Each activity

- Reinforces a key math skill

- Develops following-directions skills

- Can be completed multiple times with different outcomes

- Requires little to no teacher prep

Managing Editor: Lynn Drolet

Editorial Team: Becky S. Andrews, Diane Badden, Catherine Broome-Kehm, Kimberley Bruck, Karen A. Brudnak, Pam Crane, Chris Curry, Laura Del Prete, Pierce Foster, Tazmen Hansen, Marsha Heim, Lori Z. Henry, Troy Lawrence, Debra Liverman, Kitty Lowrance, Gerri Primak, Mark Rainey, Greg D. Rieves, Hope Rodgers, Rebecca Saunders, Donna K. Teal, Rachael Traylor, Sharon M. Tresino, Zane Williard

www.themailbox.com

©2011 The Mailbox® Books
All rights reserved.
ISBN10 #1-56234-988-0 • ISBN13 #978-1-56234-988-2

Printed in the United States
10 9 8 7 6 5 4 3 2 1

HPS22

Table of Contents

So many skills!

38 ways to give skill practice a new look!

Each activity is skill based.

Step-by-step instructions are student friendly.

Plane Shapes

What You Need

paper

crayons

What You Do

1. Think about a picture you can draw with these shapes.

circle   square   triangle   rectangle

2. Draw the picture.

3. Write.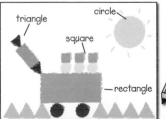

No photocopying is needed!

Supersimple Center Setup

1. Tear out the activity.

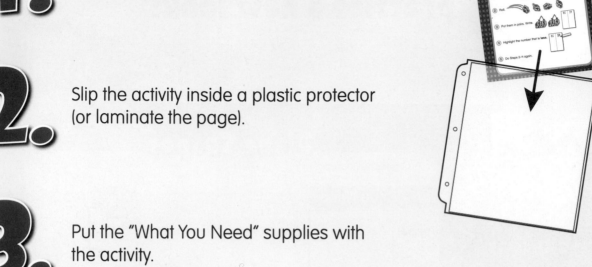

2. Slip the activity inside a plastic protector (or laminate the page).

3. Put the "What You Need" supplies with the activity.

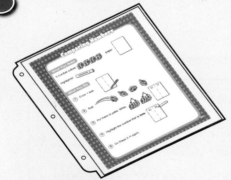

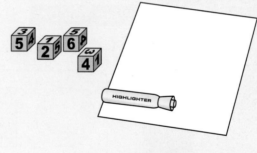

How can I use the activities?

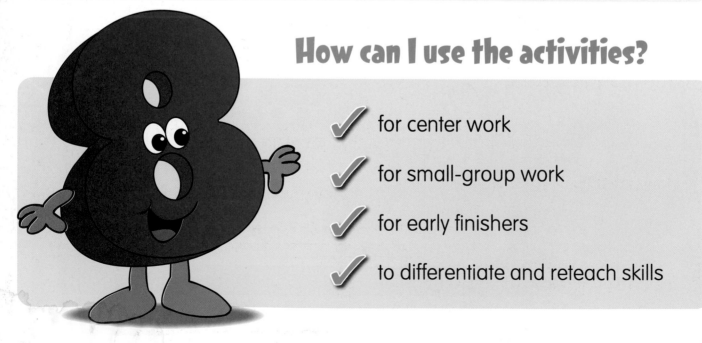

✓ for center work

✓ for small-group work

✓ for early finishers

✓ to differentiate and reteach skills

Building Sets

What You Need

stamp

ink pad

paper

die

What You Do

less		more

(1) Draw 2 lines. Write.

(2) Roll.

(3) Stamp.

less		more
	☺ ☺ ☺	

(4) Stamp 1 **less**.

less		more
☺	☺ ☺ ☺	

(5) Stamp 1 **more**.

less		more
☺ ☺	☺ ☺ ☺	☺ ☺ ☺ ☺

(6) Flip. Do Steps 1–5 again.

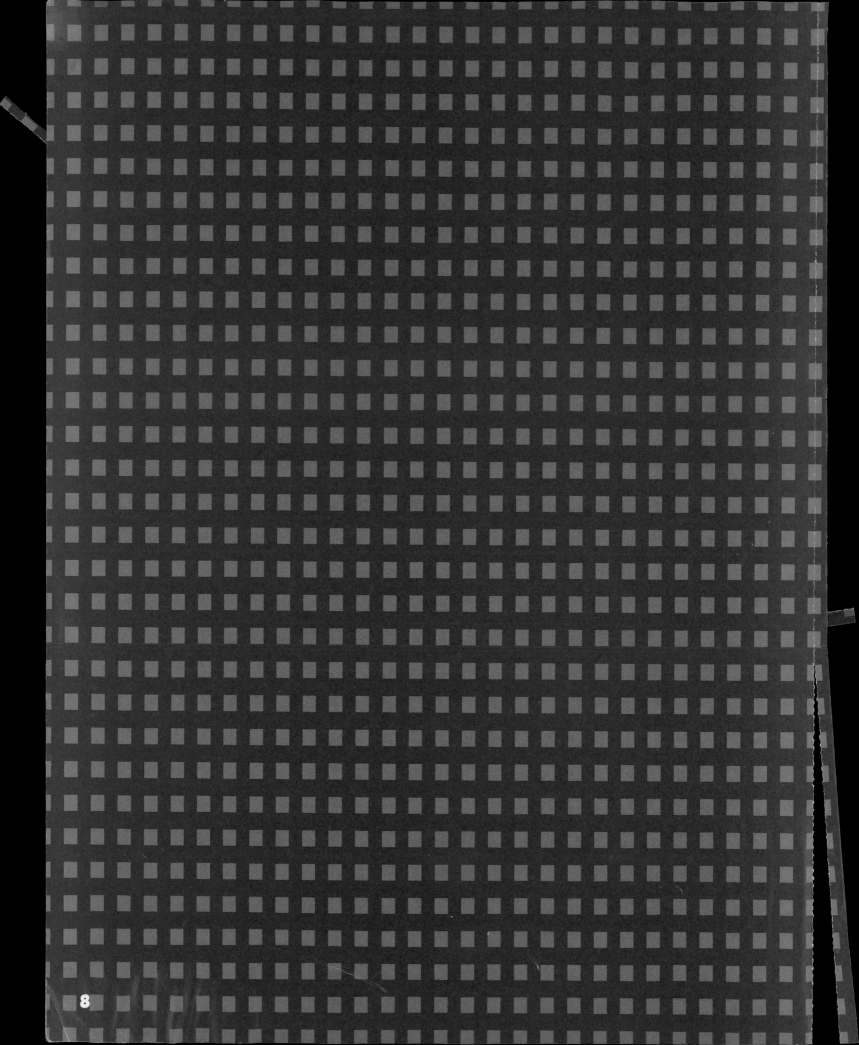

Addition to 12

What You Need

dominoes

paper

What You Do

1. Draw 1 line.

2. Put. Write. Add.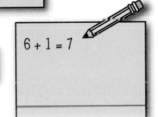

3. Turn. Write. Add.

   6 + 1 = 7
   1 + 6 = 7

4. Turn. Write. Add.

   6 + 1 = 7   6
                + 1
   1 + 6 = 7   7

5. Turn. Write. Add.

   6 + 1 = 7   6   1
                + 1 + 6
   1 + 6 = 7   7   7

6. Do Steps 2–5 again.

Addition to 18

What You Need

green number cards
  0–9 in a bag

pink number cards
  0–9 in a bag

paper

What You Do

(1) Number your paper.

(2) Shake.

(3) Take 1 card from each bag.

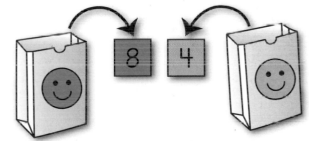

(4) Write. Add.

1. 8 + 4 = 12
2.
3.
4.

(5) Put the cards back.

(6) Do Steps 2–5 again.

18

Concept of Subtraction

What You Need

12 counters in a bag labeled with the numbers shown

die

paper

What You Do

1. Draw 2 lines.

2. Copy a number. Put.

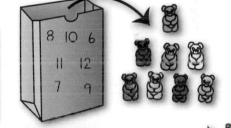

3. Roll. Write. Take away.

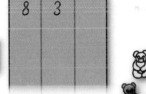

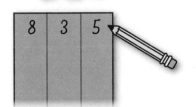

4. Count. Write.

5. Put the counters back.

6. Do Steps 2–5 again.

Subtraction to 6

What You Need

6 pom-poms in a bowl

6 cups

die

paper

What You Do

(1) Number your paper.

(2) Roll. Put that many. Write.

(3) Cover some. Write.

Take away 2.

(4) Solve.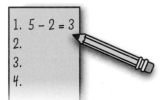

(5) Put the cups and pom-poms back.

(6) Do Steps 2–5 again.

Subtraction to 12

What You Need

number cards 4–12

paper

What You Do

(1) Number your paper.

(2) Take a card. Write. **8**

```
1. 8
2.
3.
4.
5.
```

(3) Pick a smaller number. Subtract.

| 3 | 4 | 5 | 6 | 7 | 8 | 9 |

```
1. 8 – 4
2.
3.
4.
5.
```

(4) Solve.

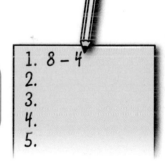

```
1. 8 – 4 =
2.
3.
4.
5.
```

(5) Do Steps 2–4 again.

Subtraction to 18

What You Need

2 large number charts as shown

1	2	3
4	5	6
7	8	9

10	11	12
13	14	15
16	17	18

beanbag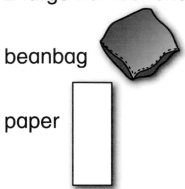

paper

What You Do

(1) Toss.

10	11	12
13	14	15
16	17	18

(2) Write the closest green number.

13

(3) Toss.

1	2	3
4	5	6
7	8	9

(4) Subtract the closest red number.

13 – 8

(5) Solve.

13 – 8 = 5

(6) Do Steps 1–5 again.

Mixed Practice

What You Need

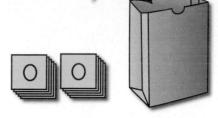

2 sets of number cards (0–9) in a bag

two-sided counter

paper

What You Do

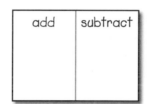

1. Draw 1 line. Write.

2. Take 2 cards.

3. Drop.

4. Write a number sentence.

   ○—add   ●—subtract

5. Put the cards back.

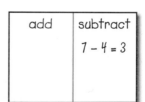

6. Do Steps 2–5 again.

Mixed Practice

What You Need

2 number cubes    crayon

paper

What You Do

① Draw 1 line. Number your paper.

② Roll.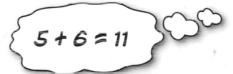

③ Add.   5 + 6 = 11

④ Write the problem below the answer.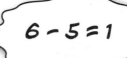

⑤ Subtract. Write.
(Start with the larger number.)   6 – 5 = 1

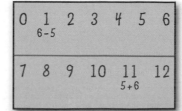

⑥ Do Steps 2–5 again.

Ordering Numbers

What You Need

number tiles   paper

What You Do

1. Draw 2 lines.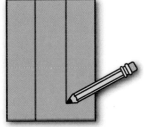

2. Put.

3. Flip 3.

4. Order from the smallest to largest number. Write.

5. Set aside the faceup numbers.

6. Do Steps 3–5 again.

Comparing Numbers

What You Need

4 number cubes    paper

highlighter

What You Do

① Draw 1 line.

② Roll.

③ Put them in pairs. Write.

65	24

④ Highlight the number that is **less.**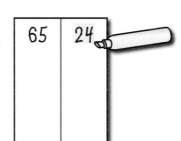

65	24

⑤ Do Steps 2–4 again.

Adding Three Numbers

What You Need

paper squares

3 dice

paper

glue  **GLUE**

What You Do

(1) Roll.

(2) Write.

(3) Glue.

(4) Write.

(5) Solve.

(6) Do Steps 1–5 again.

Two-Digit Addition

What You Need

these number cards

2 number cubes

crayon

paper

What You Do

1. Take a card. Write.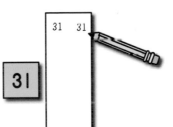

2. Roll.

3. Write. Solve.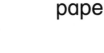

4. Move. Write. Solve.

5. Draw a line. Put the card back.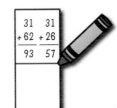

6. Do Steps 1–5 again.

Fractions

What You Need

paper shapes

paper

scissors

glue

What You Do

1) Draw 2 lines.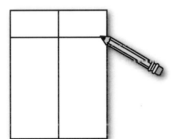

2) Write.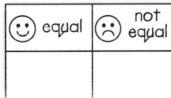

3) Take 2 matching shapes.

4) Cut 1 into **equal** parts. Glue.

5) Cut 1 into **unequal** parts. Glue.

6) Do Steps 3–5 again.

42

Fractions

What You Need

paper

crayons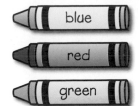

What You Do

1. Draw 2 lines.

2. Pick a fraction: $\frac{1}{2}$, $\frac{1}{3}$, or $\frac{1}{4}$.

3. Write.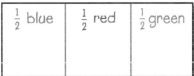

4. Draw and color to match.
   (Use these shapes to help you.)

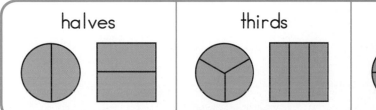

halves	thirds	fourths

5. Flip. Do Steps 1–4 again.

Writing Story Problems

What You Need

die

paper

crayons

What You Do

1. Draw 1 line.

2. Roll. Draw that many green fish. Write.

3 fish

3. Roll. Draw that many purple fish. Write.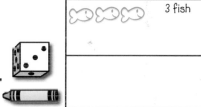

3 fish
1 more fish

4. Write.

3 fish
1 more fish
How many in all?

How many in all?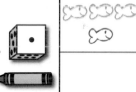

5. Solve.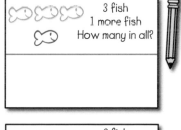

3 fish
1 more fish
How many in all?
4 fish

6. Do Steps 2–5 again.

Sorting

What You Need

attribute blocks in a container 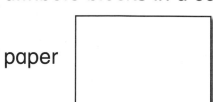   ladle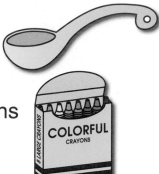

paper

crayons

What You Do

(1) Scoop.

(2) Spill.

(3) Sort by **size, shape,** or **color.**

(4) Write. Draw to show how you sorted.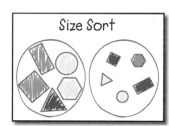

(5) Mix the shapes.

(6) Flip. Do Steps 3 and 4 again to show
    a different sort.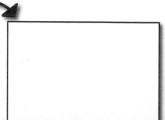

Patterns

What You Need

paper strip

crayons

What You Do

(1) Pick 2 colors.

(2) Start a pattern.

(3) Repeat the pattern 2 times.

(4) Draw details.

(5) Flip. Do Steps 1–4 again.

Patterns

What You Need

Unifix cubes, sorted in bowls

paper strip

crayons

What You Do

(1) Pick 1.

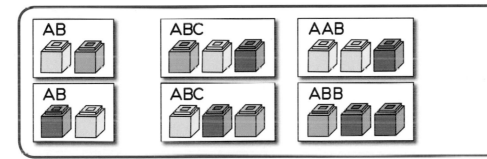

AB	ABC	AAB
AB	ABC	ABB

(2) Put.

(3) Repeat the pattern 3 more times.

(4) Draw to match.

(5) Flip. Do Steps 1–4 again.

Missing Addends

What You Need

number sentence strips

number cards 0–8 in a bag

paper

counters

What You Do

(1) Draw 2 lines. Write.

(2) Take a card. Put.

(3) Write. Solve.
(Use the counters to help you.)

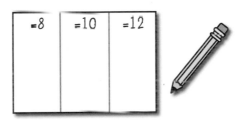

(4) Do Steps 2 and 3 two more times.

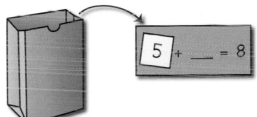

(5) Put the cards back. Do Steps 2–4 again for each number sentence.

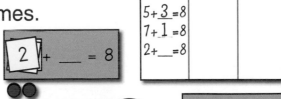

Positional Words

What You Need

word cards   over next to   ink pad

sticky notes   crayons

paper

What You Do

(1) Pick a picture. Draw it on a sticky note.

tree   flower   wagon   basket   cookie

(2) Take a card. Read. Make a thumbprint.   over

(3) Draw to make a bug.

(4) Put the sticky note on your paper.

(5) Write a sentence with the words.

The bug is over the flower.

(6) Do Steps 1–5 again.

Plane Shapes

What You Need

paper

crayons

What You Do

(1) Think about a picture you can draw with these shapes.

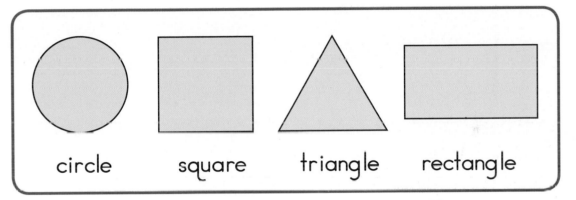

circle   square   triangle   rectangle

(2) Draw the picture.

(3) Write.

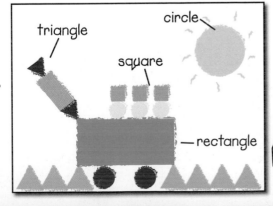

triangle
circle
square
rectangle

58

Plane Shapes

What You Need

these 6 crayons in a bag

paper

What You Do

① Write.

```
0
3
4
5
6
```

② Take a crayon. Find the same color shape.

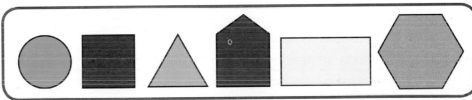

③ Count the number of sides.

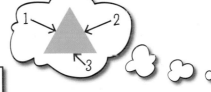

④ Draw. Color.

```
0
3
4
5
6
```

⑤ Put the crayon back.

⑥ Do Steps 2–5 again until one row has three shapes.

60

Solid Figures

What You Need

solid figures

paper

crayon

What You Do

① Draw 2 lines. Write.

② Take 1.

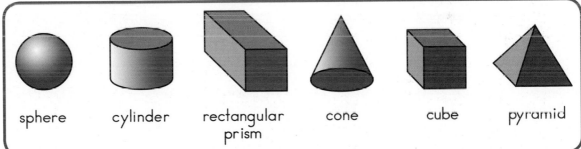

| sphere | cylinder | rectangular prism | cone | cube | pyramid |

③ Write to show if it **slides, stacks,** or **rolls.**

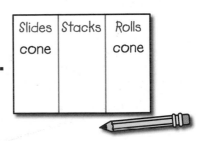

Slides	Stacks	Rolls
cone		cone

④ Do Steps 2 and 3 for each solid figure.

Measurement

What You Need

number cards 1–12

paper

ruler

crayons

What You Do

1. Take 1. Write.

2. Draw to match.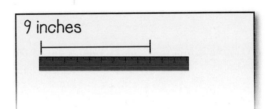

3. Do Steps 1 and 2 three more times.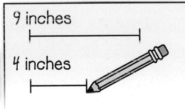

4. Draw a ☺ by the **longest** line.

5. Draw a ☺ by the **shortest** line.

6. Flip. Draw a snake that is 8 inches long.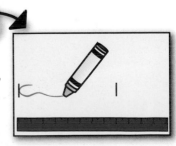

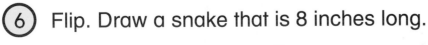

Money

What You Need

coins    paper

unwrapped crayon

What You Do

1. Draw 2 lines.

2. Look. Write 4.

| penny | quarter | 5¢ | 10¢ |
| dime | nickel | 25¢ | 1¢ |

| penny | 25¢ |
| dime | 1¢ |

3. Find the matching coin. Put.

| penny | 25¢ |
| dime | 1¢ |

4. Rub.

| penny | 25¢ |
| dime | 1¢ |

5. Do Steps 3 and 4 three more times.

Money

What You Need

2 coupons
(99¢ and under)

glue

coin manipulatives

paper

What You Do

1. Draw 1 line.

2. Glue 1 coupon.

3. Count coins to match.

4. Draw. Use the code.

1¢ penny — ①	5¢ nickel — ⑤
10¢ dime — ⑩	25¢ quarter — ㉕

   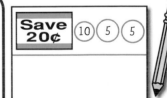

5. Do Steps 2–4 again.

Calendar

What You Need

number cards 2–30 in a bag

paper

What You Do

1 Take a card. Find the date on this calendar. Write.

March						
SUN.	MON.	TUES.	WED.	THURS.	FRI.	SAT.
		1	2	3	4	5
6	7	8	9	10	11	12
13	14	15	16	17	18	19
20	21	22	23	24	25	26
27	28	29	30	31		

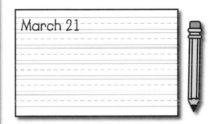

March 21

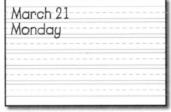

March 21
Monday

2 Write the day.

3 Write the day **before.**

4 Write the day **after.**

5 Write how many days until the 31st.

6 Do Steps 1–5 again.

Time to the Hour

What You Need

clock stamper

paper

ink pad

dice

What You Do

(1) Roll.

(2) Count. Say the number. **7.**

(3) Write the matching time. 7:00  *7 o'clock.*

(4) Stamp.  7:00

(5) Draw. 7:00

(6) Do Steps 1–5 again.

Graphing

What You Need

supply of paper squares, two colors

glue

grid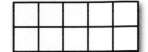

What You Do

1 Draw 1.

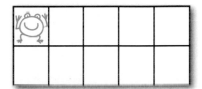

2 Count. Put to show how many.

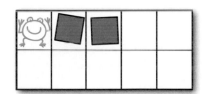

3 Glue.

4 Do Steps 1–3 again.

5 Circle to show the animal that has **more.**

Graphing

What You Need

Unifix cubes in a tub

crayons

cup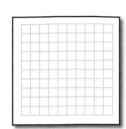

graph paper

What You Do

① Scoop.

② Sort.

③ Write.

④ Color to show how many.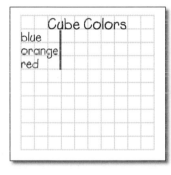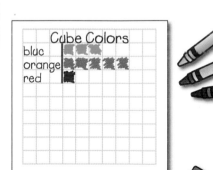

⑤ Circle the color with the **most** cubes.

⑥ Underline the color with the **fewest** cubes.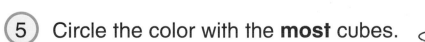

Tally Chart

What You Need

two-color counter in a cup  crayons

paper

What You Do

1. Draw 1 line.

2. Draw.

3. Spill.

4. Make a tally mark next to the matching color circle.

5. Put the counter back.

6. Do Steps 3–5 again until one color gets 10 tally marks.

Probability

What You Need

10 counters, 9 red and 1 blue, in a bag

crayons   paper

What You Do

1. Number your paper.

2. Take a counter.
   (No peeking.)

3. Take the matching color crayon. Draw.

4. Put the counter back.

5. Do Steps 2–4 again to finish your paper.

6. Empty the bag. Flip your paper.
   Write a sentence to explain.